Teaching & Learning with MAGIC

Teaching & Learning with

MAGIC

by
Charles Windley

Illustrated by John Carlance

Published by ACROPOLIS BOOKS LTD. • WASHINGTON, D.C. 20009

Printed in the United States of America by
Colortone Press Creative Graphics, Inc.
Washington, D.C. 20009

Library of Congress Cataloging in Publication Data

Windley, Charles, 1942–
  Teaching & learning with magic.

  (Invitation to learning ; 4)
  Includes index.
  1. Science—Study and teaching (Elementary)
2. Conjuring. I. Title.
LB1585.W48   372.3'5'044   76–10802
ISBN 0-87491-035-8
ISBN 0-87491-038-2 pbk.

Foreword

MY FIRST MEETING WITH Chuck Windley occurred in 1965 just after he had completed a magic show at my school. The show was sponsored by the PTA and was presented on a Saturday morning as a fund-raising project. There was so much interest that Windley ended up presenting *five* one-hour shows and we still turned people away. To me, this was more amazing than any tricks that Windley could perform in the show itself. I was a rather new principal at the time and just wasn't aware of the appeal magic has for youngsters.

When I met Windley, a personable young man in his early 20's, I learned that Marshall Elementary was just one of over 300 schools where his show would be presented that year.

The matter would have been forgotten at that point except that during the following weeks I kept finding children in the hallways and lunchroom fooling each other with simple coin tricks and puzzles. Suddenly it seemed everyone wanted to grow up to be a magician! I learned that every book on the subject had been checked out of our school library. I learned from the teachers that many book reports and science projects were suddenly taking on a magic theme.

Several years later, while writing my INVITATION TO LEARNING series, I remembered this experience and decided that magic would be a good subject for a learning center. I wanted to include this in my series but didn't have the basic knowledge of magic necessary. It was about this time, in 1973, that Windley appeared in my life again, this time to give a performance at another school where I was the principal.

I explained my concept to Windley and gave him copies of my INVITATION TO LEARNING, Volumes 1 and 2. He became excited over the idea but carried it a step further by explaining that much magic is based on scientific or mathematical principles. He felt that non-productive "fun" tricks which can be found in any school library should be left out, and only those stunts which have definite educational value included. The result is the book that you now hold in your hands.

Teachers can use this book to teach a variety of subjects to both motivate and direct students towards specific learning tasks. Parents, likewise, can make effective use of the book in much the same way. By offering the projects to children on a rainy day or while sick in bed, parents can be sure that their children's time will be used constructively.

Ralph Claude Voight

Contents

1 Fun

2 Science

Memory

Math

Perception

Skill

Creativity

Holidays

Introduction

I HAVE BEEN ASKED to write a textbook that will be used to teach magic in schools.

Over the past year I have slipped this statement into various conversations with two basic results. People not acquainted with today's educational needs look at me rather blankly and wonder "why?" or "what's the point?" Teachers, principals and others in the education field, on the other hand, become quite excited, and their enthusiasm often exceeds even my own.

I have even been surprised to meet many elementary school teachers who are already using magic in their class, although in most cases they had come up with the idea completely on their own and showed surprise that a formal book was being prepared on the subject. Their progress and ability to use magic as a learning tool, they admitted, was limited by their own lack of knowledge of the art.

Let me admit that I have no formal training in education. I am not a teacher, although I have conducted a few classes in magic as entertainment both for youngsters and adults. I am by profession a performer. I tour an illusion show throughout the United States for the sole purpose of entertainment. I have observed, however, that professional magicians view life and their surroundings a little differently than most people. Magicians seldom completely trust their senses because they are well aware of how the senses can be fooled. To be a good magician requires not only a pleasant personality but a thorough knowledge of math and the sciences as well as human nature. Magicians learn to question and examine almost everything.

We are taught that a ball rolls down a hill and that is that. This sourcebook, however, teaches not one but two ways to make a ball roll up a hill. In doing so we have not contradicted the laws of physics but only used these laws in a different way. It is the purpose of this book to introduce such creative thinking into a child's life.

Just as a performing magician's end purpose is fun, this

book is presented as fun. All slight-of-hand tricks and the like have been left out. Every trick or stunt is based on a known principle of science or math, and it is these principles that the teacher should keep in mind and that the student should discover.

Why magic in a classroom? Because it can be used as a valuable tool to make children ask questions and seek answers. Isn't that what learning is all about?

How to
Use this Book

IN THE BEGINNING I KNEW very little about "open classrooms" or "learning centers," and my introduction to the subject came from reading the three volumes of *Invitation to Learning* by Ralph Voight (Acropolis Books Ltd., Washington, D.C.). I would suggest that you review these publications if you are not completely familiar with the concept.

From that point, I spent many hours visiting open classrooms throughout the country. I only wish such a concept was in operation when I was a student, as I am a product of the "monkey see-monkey do" system of the fifties. The only creative thing I remember doing in school was using my knowledge of math to calculate how many days I had left before I would graduate.

I then had Mr. Voight and other educators make up a workable format for this book before I filled in the blank pages. I sifted through thousands of magic tricks before I came up with the seventy-five contained herein. Because I feel that all classroom time is valuable, I wanted each trick to have a value of its own. Every project sheet furthers the student's knowledge. Sometimes a trick will give the student a better understanding of math or science. Sometimes, by performing these stunts, the student will develop a better understanding of communication or human nature.

To help you I have categorized these tricks. Your responsibility as teacher is to pair the stunt with the right student to help him with his particular needs. A student who constantly forgets his lunch money should be offered the project sheets on memory, while the student who finds math a boring subject should be offered sections from math.

We cannot do something well unless we enjoy doing it. One major purpose of this book is to prove that learning is indeed fun.

How to
Set Up a Magic
Learning Center

ALL THAT IS NEEDED FOR a Magic Learning Center is a table set in the corner of the room. A three-fold screen of cardboard is set on the table. This can be easily decorated by you, or several students can do it as an art project. "Magic" or "Be A Magician" should be written at the top of the screen in large letters. Because the project sheets sometimes refer to the screen, it should contain the following:

1. The right panel should contain a drawing of a magician's arm. His sleeve is actually a packet made from construction paper, and it is this packet that contains the project sheets.

2. The left panel should contain a top hat also made into a packet. Some project sheets require the student to complete a written work assignment to be left in the magic hat where you can look them over later for review.

3. The bottom of the center panel should have a mirror pasted on it so the student can see the reflection of his hands or of other objects as he works at the table.

4. The following should be printed somewhere on the screen:

   Remember the magician's code:

   1. DON'T reveal the secret of a trick, even to your best friend.
   2. DON'T perform the same trick twice before the same audience.
   3. DON'T do any trick for friends until you have practiced it.
   4. DON'T interfere with others when they do magic. Cooperate with them as you would want them to do if you were performing.

Since you will know ahead of time which students are assigned to work at the Magic Learning Center, you should place the appropriate project sheet in the magic sleeve. You should also make sure that the necessary materials are available on the table. Check the appendix at the end of the book for a list of needed materials for each project. Most materials are readily available in the classroom, although occasionally an inexpensive item will have to be brought from home or purchased.

Since a student is never required to cut or draw directly on a project sheet, these sheets can be used many times.

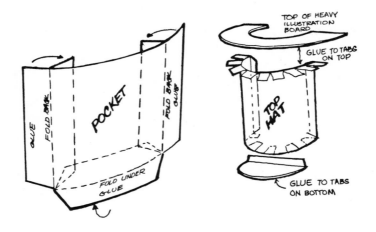

Using
The Magic Learning
Center

LEARN A FEW MAGIC TRICKS YOURSELF from the "Fun" section of the book and perform them before the entire class but, of course, don't tell how the tricks were done. "Houdini, Jr." and "The Magic Balloon" would be good stunts to perform.

Then have a class discussion on magic and magicians. You will be amazed at how much the students already know about the subject. Have a few students describe magic shows they have seen, either in person or on television, and invite some students to come before the class and perform any magic that they already know. Have a deck of cards handy for this discussion since there are always several students in a class that know a few card tricks.

Be sure, in the discussion, to explain that magic is based on secrecy and that good magicians never tell how their tricks are done. Why is this? Would magic be fun if you knew the secret? Read them the "Magician's Code."

Explain to the class that you have set up a Magic Learning Center and show the center to the class. It is available to anyone who would like to be a magician. All they have to do is promise to be a good magician and never reveal any secrets learned at the center.

Students wishing to participate are to check with you and sign up for a particular time on a particular day. Prior to that time you are to select a project from this workbook which most fits that student's needs and place a project sheet in the "magician's sleeve." Since there are many projects in each section, a student can return to the Magic Learning Center many times. A student should never be given more than one project sheet on any given day.

THE AUDIENCE

Some projects are completely self contained and are solely between the student and the project sheet. Others, however, are to be performed. First make sure that the magician has read and studied the trick and practiced a few times before he demonstrates his newly acquired mystery. You can then have him perform for you or an aide or another student. It will not be necessary for the aide to be aware of the trick or its secret beforehand and would even be preferable if the aide knew nothing at all about the trick to be performed. Thus an aide will not have to pretend to be surprised. The students should also be encouraged to perform for their parents at home that evening.

Or, upon occasion, arrangements can be made for the new magician to perform before the entire class. It is amazing how students who are normally quite shy about giving book reports, etc. become great show offs while making a pencil float in the air.

You may even set aside an hour once a week or so for a magic show in which students take turns getting up before the class to perform their favorite trick from the Magic Learning Center. This could be considered part of public speaking. The "magician's code" is important here and care should be given to see that no student is heckled by his classmates should he make a mistake.

THE APPENDIX

On occasion a project sheet does not give a student the secret or solution but challenges him to discover the secret for himself. To help you as a teacher the proper solutions are provided in the appendix. As a footnote to this I might inject that as a professional magician, I am well aware that children are much harder to fool with magic than adults. My only explanation is that a child's mind is uncluttered, and he can often see right to the point while an adult's higher knowledge stands in the way. In presenting these project sheets to various schools for testing before inclusion in this book, I was amused to find examples in which students quickly solved problems on their own that their teachers to this day do not yet understand. It is my feeling that you, as an adult, will learn much from your students with these experiments. Please don't hesitate to ask your junior magician about anything in this book that you do not understand.

Fun 1

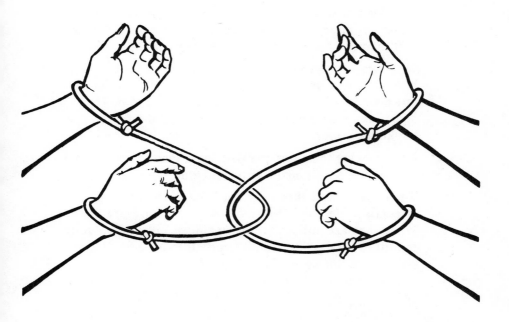

Houdini was perhaps the most famous magician of all time. He died in 1926 on Halloween. He could make elephants disappear and he could walk through a brick wall, but his most famous magic was his escape trick. He performed many times with circuses, and this trick as well as others in this book would be fun to use if your school ever presents an amateur circus. It seemed that no matter how people tied Houdini's hands he would always get loose. Here is one of his famous escapes. See if you can figure out Houdini's secret?

1. This requires two people so you will need a partner. You will also need two pieces of rope or string.

2. Have your partner tie one end of a string around his left wrist. It should be tied loosely like a bracelet but not so loosely that he can slip his hand out.

3. The other end of the string should be tied around his right wrist.

4. Now it is your turn. Tie another piece of string around your left wrist, then loop your string through his before tying your right wrist.

5. The problem is for you and your partner to separate your-selves without untying the knots or cutting the string. It *can* be done.

Strong Man

Did you ever wonder what it would be like to be the strongest person in the world? One way to find out is to spend several hours a day developing your muscles. Another way is to use your head . . . and a little trickery.

1. For this test of strength you will need a good quality paper napkin or paper towel. Roll the napkin into a tight tube and then twist it many times like a rope.

2. Give the napkin to someone and challenge him/her to hold each end and pull the napkin apart. This looks easy but even a strong grown-up will not be able to pull it apart. It seems that the harder they pull, the tighter the napkin becomes.

3. Now imagine their surprise when you take the very same napkin and pull it apart with almost no effort at all.

4. The secret is that they have tried to use their physical strength while you have used your knowledge of science. While they are pulling, wet your fingers either with your mouth or by dipping them secretly into a glass of water. Now when the napkin is returned to you take it by the center. Your index finger and thumb will wet the center and cause the paper fibers to weaken at that point. Now it will be easy to grab both ends and pull the napkin apart.

5. If people see you wet your fingers then they will know that they have been tricked. If you do not want to put your fingers in your mouth and you find it difficult to slip your fingers into a glass without being seen, then you might wet a piece of sponge or another rolled up piece of napkin before the experiment and keep this in your pocket. It should be easy to place your hand in your pocket and squeeze the paper or sponge without getting caught.

The Magic Rolling Crayon

Can you make up a story about a magic rolling crayon? Give a crayon to a friend and tell him a make-believe story about how the crayon rolls all by itself. Of course your friend won't believe you at first, but then to prove your story, place the crayon on a table and run your index finger on your sleeve. As you touch the table several inches in front of the crayon it begins to move all by itself and rolls right to your finger.

Your story can be spooky or funny or serious. After you tell your story, here is the real reason that the crayon rolled:

1. You will need a fairly new crayon that is perfectly round. Place it on the table in front of you parallel to the edge of the table.

2. Now rub your finger on your sleeve and place it in front of the crayon. The rubbing doesn't mean anything at all but is just done to distract your friend's attention.

3. As soon as your finger touches the table, quietly blow on the table just behind the crayon. It is actually your breath that makes the crayon roll.

4. When you practice this you will learn that you do not have to blow very hard but remember that you do not actually blow the crayon. You blow *behind* the crayon so that your breath bounces off the table and pushes the crayon from underneath.

5. You must also remember not to make a face when blowing that would give the secret away.

6. Practice by yourself first and then try this magic on a friend.

7. What story did you make up about the crayon. Write your story on a piece of paper and leave it in the magic hat.

Four Aces

Did you know that playing cards were invented by magicians? The cards that we use today were designed by Egyptian magicians many centuries ago and were designed after our solar system. There are 52 cards in a deck because we have 52 weeks in a year. There are two colors for night and day. The four suits are the symbol of the four seasons—spring, summer, winter and fall. Also there are exactly 12 picture cards because we have 12 months in a year.

If you add up all the numbers in a deck of cards (using 11 for jacks, 12 for queens and 13 for kings) the total is 365, representing the 365 days in a year. The joker or extra card represents leap year or the extra day every four years.

In many card games, the most valuable cards are the four aces. Here is an amazing magic trick that you can perform with a deck of cards:

1. Hand a deck of cards to a friend and have him shuffle them. Then have him hand you the deck behind your back. Even though you cannot see the cards you quickly find the four aces.

2. Like all good magic, the secret is really easy. Before performing the trick remove the four aces from the deck and place them in your back pocket.

3. When you give your friend the deck to shuffle, don't tell him what you are going to do and he will have no reason to count the cards or check to see if the aces are there.

4. When he hands you the deck, simply turn around and face him so that he cannot see what you are doing behind your back. Reach in your back pocket and hand him the aces one at a time, then give him the rest of the deck to examine.

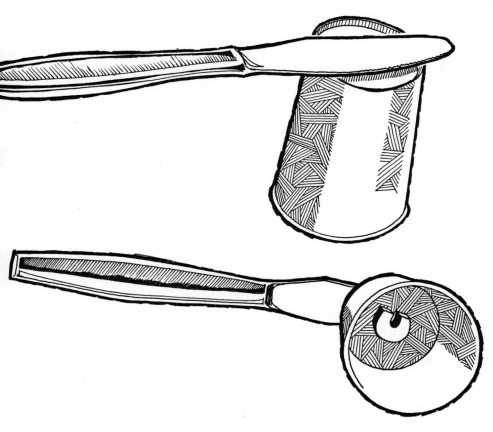

Defying Gravity

1. For this magic trick you will need a metal table knife, a paper cup and a small magnet.

2. Secretly place the magnet in the cup. Show the cup and knife to your friends but stand back away from them so that they do not see the magnet in the cup.

3. Hold the knife by the handle and carefully sit the cup on the blade. While pretending to balance the cup move it about until the knife is directly under the magnet.

4. Let go and pretend to hypnotise the cup. Then slowly turn the knife over and the cup will stick to the knife. Be sure that you turn the cup over towards you and not away from you or your friends will see the magnet in the cup.

5. After the trick hold the mouth of the cup from underneath and lift the knife. The magnet will secretly fall into your hand.

6. Now you can pass the knife and cup to your friends to examine. While they are looking at the cup, secretly slip the magnet into your pocket.

The Magic Balloon

Did you ever see someone stick a pin in a balloon? Chances are that before the pin actually touched the balloon you held your hands over your ears and made a funny face. People hate to hear a balloon pop. Wouldn't it be great if someone could invent a balloon that didn't pop! Here is a way to keep a balloon from bursting . . . by magic.

1. You need several round balloons and several pins or needles. Also you will need a roll of transparent tape. This trick works best with a tape that is very sticky.

2. Blow up a balloon and tie a knot in the end. Now stick several squares of tape on the balloon in different places. Make sure that you stick them on carefully so that there is no air between the tape and balloon. If you stand a few feet away when performing this magic, the tape will not be seen. (People will be too afraid to stand close anyway when they see what you are about to do.)

3. Show the balloon to some friends and slowly stick a pin into the balloon. Pretend that you are sticking the pin at a random spot but really stick it through the center of one of the pieces of tape. The pin goes through the tape and balloon but the balloon will not pop because the plastic tape holds it together. Now remove the pin and the escaping air will force the glue from the tape into the empty space and plug up the hole. This is much the same way that tubeless tires on automobiles seal themselves when a nail is removed.

4. Now stick the pin into another spot on the balloon where you have another piece of tape. To add some fun to the magic you should repeat some strange magic words everytime you do this. You can tell your friends that the balloon will not pop as long as you remember to say the magic words.

5. Give someone else the pin and have him try. Of course he doesn't know the secret so when he sticks the pin into the balloon it will pop with a bang.

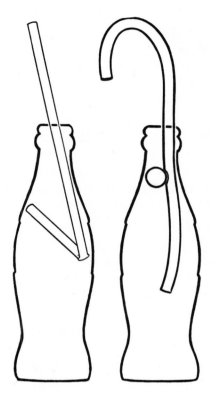

The Genie in the Bottle

Magicians are often accused of having invisible helpers. Here is a way that you can introduce your invisible helper to your friends and have him perform a few experiments. Since genies live in bottles, show your friends a soft drink bottle that has been painted so they cannot see inside. "Even genies like a little privacy once in a while," you explain.

To prove that he is in there, you place a soda straw in the bottle and tell him to grab it and hold on tight. He holds so tight that you can pick up the bottle by the straw.

Next you place the end of a rope in the bottle and swing the bottle back and forth by the rope. When you tell your genie to let go, however, the rope easily comes out of the bottle. This only works for you of course because he is your genie. You can give the rope and bottle to your friends but they will try without success.

1. First you will need an empty soft drink bottle. It must be painted so that the inside of the bottle cannot be seen. You can use a brush and paint the outside if you like but this can be messy and takes a long time. The easiest way is to pour about an inch of paint into the empty bottle, cover the top and shake until the paint has completely covered

the inside. Then pour the excess paint back into the can. Make sure that the paint is completely dry before continuing with the trick. While waiting for the inside to dry you might take a small brush and another color and paint some mystic symbols on the outside of the bottle.

2. You will also need a drinking straw (a paper straw works much better than a plastic one), a piece of thin rope such as window sash cord (about 12 inches long) and a small cork or rubber ball that is a little more than half the diameter of the mouth of your bottle.

3. Show the empty bottle to your friends and let them examine it. They can peek inside through the top if they like but warn them not to turn the bottle upside down or your genie may fall out. Take the bottle back from your friends and stick the straw in a few times, telling the genie to grab it but of course nothing happens.

4. Sit the bottle on the table and pretend to get mad with the genie. As you talk to the genie, secretly bend the straw a few inches from the end. For the trick to work, the bent part of the straw must be a little longer than the bottle is wide. Holding your left hand in front of the bottle, insert the folded straw with your right hand. Once inside the bottle, the straw will open and wedge at a cross-angle thus serving as a brace so you can carefully lift the bottle.

5. To make the genie release the straw, hold the bottle with your left hand and jerk the straw hard with your right hand. Your friends can now try this but unless they saw you secretly bend the straw they won't be able to lift the bottle.

6. Now give them the rope to examine. While they are looking at the rope, reach in your pocket for the little ball or cork, and secretly drop it into the bottle.

7. Place the bottle back on the table and, when your friends return the rope, insert one end into the bottle. With the rope inside, turn the bottle upside down and rub the bottom. The rubbing has nothing to do with the trick but because you have the bottle upside down the ball or cork will roll down and wedge between the rope and the narrow opening. Give the rope a little tug to make the wedge tight and you can swing the bottle back and forth on the rope.

8. Sit the bottle on the table with force and push the rope in a bit and the little ball will release and fall back to the bottom. The rope can now easily be removed.

9. To get rid of the secret ball hold the bottle by the neck and again turn it upside down showing your friends where they must rub. While you are talking the ball will roll into your hand and you can give them the empty bottle. As they are looking at it, secretly put the little ball back into your pocket.

Science 2

The Floating Needle

1. You will need a glass or bowl of water, several sewing needles and a pen and paper. Every time a question is asked, write your answers on the paper. When the experiment is over, sign your paper and leave it in the magic hat.

2. The magic is to try and float the needle on the water. Try this by yourself and see if you can do it. Make sure that you dry the needle completely after each try because a wet needle will not float.

3. There are many different ways to make the needle float on the water. What do you know about science that will help you? Maybe you will invent a new way that has never been done before.

4. For the magic hat, make a list of all the ways you tried. Did they work?

5. Try with a different shaped glass or bowl. Did this make it easier?

6. What is surface tension?

7. Get a fresh glass of water and a new needle and try this: Place a small piece of paper on the water. The paper should be about one inch wide and just a little longer than the needle. Now drop the needle on the paper. Soon the paper, as it gets wet, will sink to the bottom and leave the needle floating on top. Now you have successfully performed the trick. Do you know why the needle is floating?

8. Another way to make the needle float is to lay the needle across the teeth of a fork and carefully lower the fork into the water but this is hard to do. Can you do it?

9. If you try the above experiments with a straight pin they will not work. The real secret to the floating needle trick is the 'eye' in the needle. The needle can never float if there is water in the eye, but if the little hole is completely dry then it will float every time provided you do not break the surface tension of the water. Why do you think this is true?

Poof!

A good magician always understands how and why his magic works. I will teach you to perform a trick, but you must figure out the real secret for yourself.

1. You will need an empty glass, a nickel, and a paper match furnished by the teacher.

2. Balance the coin on its edge and then carefully balance a paper match on top of the coin. This requires a steady hand but isn't as hard as it sounds. It will help if you bend the match slightly. Now turn the glass over and cover the match and coin.

3. Without touching the glass, the coin, the match, or the table, the trick is to make the match jump off of the nickel without affecting the balancing nickel.

4. No, it is not impossible to do if you are a magician. Try to do it before reading the answer.

5. Take a pocket comb and run the comb through your hair several times. Then hold the teeth of the comb close to the glass near the match and move it up and down. The match will jump off of the nickel and do a little dance.

6. Now you have performed some amazing magic but can you figure out why the match really jumped off of the nickel? Write your answer and leave it in the magic hat.

Falling for Science

1. For this stunt you will need a coin such as a quarter or a half dollar and a piece of paper. Cut the paper into a circle or disc smaller than the coin.

2. Hold both objects over a table and drop both at the same time. You will notice that the coin hits the table first. Is this because the coin is heavier than the paper?

3. Once there was a cowboy magician who fooled other cowboys with this trick. He would bet them that he could drop the coin and the paper in such a way that both would hit the table at exactly the same time. Although the other cowboys would make sure that he dropped the paper and the coin from the same height, he always won his bet. Without using any other objects except the coin and the paper, see if you can figure out the magician's secret.

4. A good solution to this problem would be to wet the paper and make it stick to the coin but that is not what the magician did. Instead he used a simple principle of science.

5. Once you are able to make the coin and paper land at the same time, write your secret on a piece of paper and leave it in the magic hat.

6. Hint: It is a law of physics that all objects fall at the same velocity, regardless of their weight.

7. Need another hint? The factor to overcome is air resistance.

How to Make a Rainbow

Have you ever seen a rainbow? Rainbows sometimes appear in the sky just after a rainfall and can be very pretty with their many colors. There was a time when people didn't understand what caused a rainbow and thought that they were the result of magic. Some would travel many miles to find the end of the rainbow but of course they never succeeded because rainbows are only an illusion.

Here is a way to make a rainbow of your own:

1. Get two pieces of glass—picture frame glass will do—and wet the sides with water and then hold them together.

2. Now light a candle. If you look through the glass at the flame of the candle, you will be amazed and pleased with the rainbow colored fringes that appear between the glass.

3. This is the effect of moisture intermixed with air. Just as you see a rainbow caused by the moisture in the air reflected by the sun, so do you get this same effect by wetting the glass.

Spilling the Beans

1. Here is a stunt that looks impossible and indeed your friends won't be able to do it, but like most good magic it is easy once you know the secret.

2. You will need an empty soft drink bottle, a dried bean such as a navy bean and a wide bangle bracelet. These are bracelets that do not open, but are continuous loops of metal or plastic and slip over the hand.

3. Balance the bracelet over the mouth of the bottle and then balance the bean on top of the bracelet directly above the mouth of the bottle. The bean should be centered exactly so that when it falls in a straight line it will fall into the bottle. This is exactly what you are going to try and do by taking your finger and knocking the bracelet away.

4. You can try this several times but you will learn that no matter how quickly you knock the bracelet away, the bean will always miss the bottle. The stunt appears to be pretty hard.

5. The secret is not to hit the bracelet on the outside, but to strike it on the far inside (at point 'B' in the illustration).

6. The reason for this is that the sudden removal of the bracelet leaves the bean unsupported and it falls straight down into the bottle. When you hit the outside, however, the bracelet turns as it moves away and pushes the bean away from the bottle.

Salt and Pepper

1. Pour a mound of salt on a piece of paper. Now add some pepper to the pile and mix the two together. The problem, Mr. Magician, is to separate the salt and pepper. Can you do it?

2. There are several solutions to this problem. See if you can figure it out by yourself before reading the answer.

3. One solution is to dump the mixture into a glass of water. The salt quickly sinks to the bottom and desolves while the pepper floats on top.

4. Another way would be to take a pocket comb and run it through your hair several times, then hold the comb close to, but not touching, the pile. One of the two seasonings will jump out of the pile and cling to the comb. I'm not telling which one. You will have to try this yourself to find out.

5. These are two ways to separate the salt and pepper. Can you think of another? If you can, leave your new solution in the magic hat. Maybe you will invent a new way that has never been done before.

Looping an Ice Cube

1. All right cowboy, make a lasso or a loop on the end of a piece of string.

2. Now take an ice cube and drop it into a glass of water. From now on you are not allowed to touch either the glass, the water or the ice cube with your fingers.

3. Using the loop of string, lift the cube out of the water. Of course you must do it before the ice melts or you will have nothing to lift.

4. Did you try it? Ice can be pretty slippery can't it? It can be done, of course, but in addition to the string you also have to use your head . . . to think with, that is.

5. What have you learned in science that would make it possible to accomplish this trick?

6. Need a hint? Is it possible to melt the ice enough for the string to go inside and then refreeze the cube around the string? That is the real secret but how?

7. Still need a hint? How do people melt the ice that forms on sidewalks in the winter?

8. If you really give up then you will have to ask your teacher but the answer is so simple that you'll be mad when you are told.

The Magic Match

1. Here is a neat mind reading stunt that you can perform by yourself. You give your friend several wooden matches that are exactly alike. One of the matches, however, has a pencil mark on the side. Your friend mixes the matches and hands them to you under a table where you can't see them. Without looking you always find the match with the pencil mark.

2. To prepare for this trick you will need several wooden matches, two pairs of pliers and a couple of small pieces of cloth.

3. Before performing the trick, prepare one of the matches by wrapping each end with a piece of cloth to protect it and then hold each end with a pair of pliers. Slowly twist the match by twisting one end forward and the other end backward as far as you can without breaking it. Now twist the match back to its original shape. Do this several times until you have weakened the match so much that you can twist it with your fingers. (The purpose of the cloth is to keep the pliers from making teeth marks in the wood.) After preparing the match in this way mark it with a pencil and place it with the others. Now you are ready to perform the magic.

4. When your friend hands you the matches under the table, twist each one until you find the match that gives when twisted. This, of course, is the match that is marked.

5. After the trick you can let your friends examine the matches but no one will think to twist them sideways. This is a great trick based on the scientific principle that wood fibers weaken under constant strain. You are dealing with tension instead of just pliability because if you bend the matches the other way as if to break them you will notice no difference. This principle is important because it explains why accidents sometimes happen even though the materials have been tested for strength. Metals as well as wood can weaken under tension which explains why a bridge will occasionally break or an airplane wing will break.

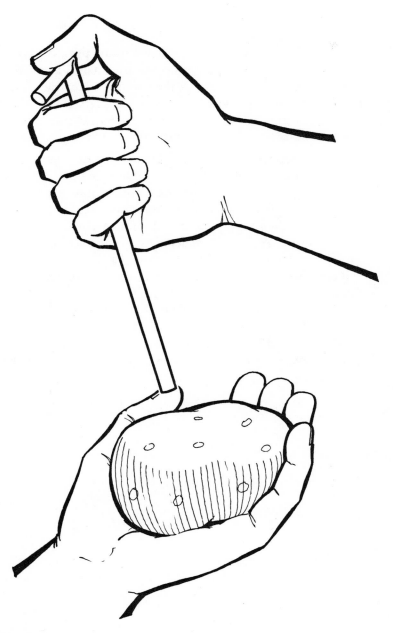

The Sword and the Stone

Have you ever heard the story about how King Arthur became a king? It seems that some magicians had a sword embedded in a stone and announced that the one person smart enough or strong enough to remove the sword would become the next king. Everyone from across the land tried but it was little Arthur who removed it with ease. The story is an interesting one, and there is probably a book on King Arthur in your library.

The real mystery, however, is how the magicians were able to stab the sword into the stone in the first place and that is what this magic trick is all about. For a sword you can use a paper drinking straw and for the stone you can demonstrate on a raw potato.

1. Let your friends examine the straw and the potato and then take the objects back into your own hands and jab the straw completely through the potato. Your friends can try but unless they know the simple secret they will accomplish nothing more than bending the straw. Try this yourself before reading the secret.

2. A straw is too weak to be jabbed through a raw potato by itself but it can be done if you give it a little help. Before performing the trick, secretly bend about an inch of the top of the straw inward and flatten it against the thumb and fingers, then hold your thumb on top of the crease as in the picture. All that remains is to give the straw a straight direct thrust against the side of the potato and it will continue completely through and come out the other side.

3. Now you know how to do this trick but can you figure out why it works? What happens inside the straw when you bend the end? Figure out the real secret and explain it on another sheet of paper. Sign your paper and leave it in the magic hat.

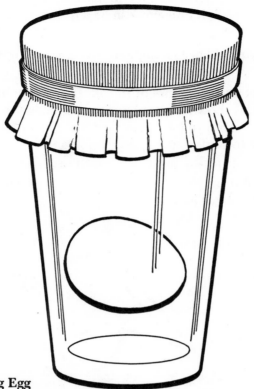

The Dancing Egg

1. To perform this simple trick you will need a rubber band, a glossy or slick piece of paper (a page from a quality magazine will do), a large drinking glass and an empty egg shell.

2. To obtain an empty egg shell, take a real egg and carefully punch a small hole in each end with a needle or straight pin. The best way to empty the contents of the egg is to place your mouth over one of the holes and suck the egg through the hole. Raw eggs (with no cracks) are very good for you but some people do not like the taste. Another way is to blow into the egg and force the contents through the other hole into a glass.

3. Now place the empty egg into a clean glass and cover the mouth of the glass with the paper, putting the rubber band around the glass making a drum head.

4. When you push the paper with a slight touch of your finger, the egg will rise up and float in the air. When you release your finger it will return to the bottom of the glass. With a little practice you can make the egg perform a little dance by tapping on the paper.

5. The secret behind this magic is that when you push down on the paper the displaced air in the glass will force its way into the egg shell thereby making it jump or rise in the glass.

Rolling up a Hill

1. Do you think it is possible to make an object roll UP an incline? Here is how you can be a real magician and defy the laws of gravity.

2. First you will need a slight incline. An easy way to make this is to lean a large book on another book.

3. Now you need a spool of thread. Lay the spool on the incline as shown in the picture and pull on the thread. The spool will not roll down as expected but will roll up the incline towards you.

4. Why does the spool roll up instead of down? If you can figure out the secret, write it on a piece of paper and leave it in the magic hat.

5. Here is another way to make an object roll up a hill. You will need two funnels with their wide mouths glued together. Now make an incline by folding a piece of heavy cardboard and drawing a pattern on it like that in the picture. Cut out the pattern and place it on a table. The cardboard is in a 'V' with the open ends a few inches apart.

6. Place the funnel at the bottom of the incline and it will roll to the top all by itself. Doesn't this look spooky?

7. If you can figure out the secret to this trick, write it down also and leave it in the magic hat.

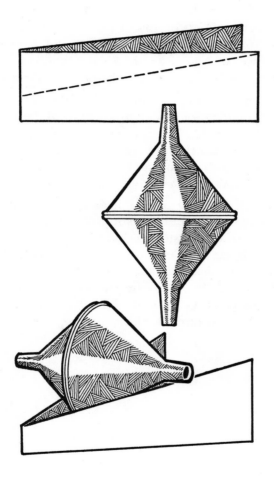

The Mysterious Button

1. You will need a small shirt button and a glass of carbonated water.

2. Wrap the button in a tissue and you are ready to begin. Show the button to your friends, carefully unwrapping it as if it were very valuable and mysterious.

3. Drop the button into the glass of water and, of course, it will sink to the bottom.

4. Recite some magic words and make some funny motions with your hands pretending that you are hypnotising the button. Then snap your fingers and the button will slowly begin to move and rise up to the top of the glass.

5. As the button floats on top of the water, claim that you will try to hypnotise the button again and make some more passes with your hands. Finally snap your fingers and the button will float down to the bottom of the glass.

6. You can do this several times because the button will keep rising and falling for several hours or until the carbonated water becomes flat. The magic words and waving of your hands are just for show because the button trick works by itself. You just have to watch to see when the button begins to move and snap your fingers at that time.

7. If you look carefully at the button during the trick you will notice little air bubbles sticking to it and that is the real secret to the mysterious button. Because the water is carbonated, air bubbles form on the button until so many attach that the bubbles carry the button to the top where it will float. While on top the bubbles begin to pop and the button, being heavy, sinks back to the bottom of the glass where it collects more bubbles.

Memory 3

FOUR PROJECTS:

1. Colors

2. Remember That Day

3. Calendar

4. Super Memory

Colors

1. Take three pieces of paper about two inches square and color as follows:

   > 1st—color one side *red* and the other side *green*
   > 2nd—color one side *white* and the other side *yellow*
   > 3rd—color one side *blue* and the other side *black*

2. Place the three squares on a table and tell a friend that while your back is turned, he may turn the cards over as many times as he wishes. Then he is to cover any one of the three cards with his hand, and you will turn around and tell him which color he is covering.

3. The secret is math. You mentally give a number value of 1 for each of the colors in the flag—red, white and blue. The other colors—green, yellow and black—have a number value of 0 (zero).

4. It doesn't matter how the cards are thrown down in the beginning but before you turn around, look at the colors and add their values. For example, if the colors showing were red, yellow and blue then you would remember two because $1 + 0 + 1 = 2$.

5. Turn your back and tell your friend that he can turn any card over as many times as he wishes but he can only turn one card at a time. As he makes each turn he is to say "turn!" out loud. When he is finished, he is to cover any one of the three cards with his hand so that you will not be able to see it when you face him.

6. While your back is turned, add 1 to your previous total each time your friend says the word 'turn'. When he is finished, your total will either be an odd or an even number. If it is an odd number, then there will be either 1 or all 3 of the flag colors showing. If the result is even then there will be none or 2 of the flag colors showing.

7. With this information it will be easy to tell which color he is covering simply by turning around and looking at the other two colors.

Remember That Day

Wouldn't it be great if you could figure out what day of the week a special date fell on? This not only can be fun but could also be quite useful. When studying history it would be more interesting to know that July 4, 1776, was a Thursday or that your friend was born on a Monday.

This can work in the future as well as the past. After reading this project sheet you will be able to figure out what day of the week January 12, 1984, will fall upon without looking at a calendar. The system is a little complicated but well worth the effort to learn. Here is how it works:

1. Pick a date such as the date that you were born. Forget the '19' and divide the last two digits by 4. Forget any fraction or remainder but take the whole number of your answer and add it to the last two digits of the year. Write down your total on a piece of paper.

2. Now use the following table and add the number that is beside the month in your date.

Table A

Month	Key Number
January	1
February	4
March	4
April	0 (if leap year, add 3)
May	2
June	5
July	0
August	3
September	6
October	1
November	4
December	6

3. Now add the day of the month to your total. (Example: For June *20*, 1955, you would add 20.)

4. If your date is in this century then you can skip this step. If your date is before 1900, then add the key number in this chart:

Table B

Year	Key
1900–2000	add 0
1800–1900	add 2
1752–1800	add 4
1700–1751	add 1
1600–1699	add 2

(add 2 plus 1 for each century further back from 1600)

5. Now with all of your numbers added together, divide the result by 7. The whole number in your answer is not important but the *remainder* will tell you on which day of the week your date occured. If there is no remainder, then the date was a Saturday, a remainder of 1 means the date was a Sunday, etc.

Table C

Remainder		Day of the Week
0	–	Saturday
1	–	Sunday
2	–	Monday
3	–	Tuesday
4	–	Wednesday
5	–	Thursday
6	–	Friday

6. Table B and C are easy to learn but table A will take a little practice.

7. Here is an example of how the system works. Suppose we wanted to find the day of the week for June 20, 1942.

    a. Write the last two digits   42

    b. divide by 4   10½

    c. forget any remainder, which leaves 10

    d. add this number to your year   10 + 42 = 52

    e. check table A. June is 5   52 + 5 = 57

    f. add table B (1942=0)   57 + 0 = 57

    g. add the date of the month   57 + 20 = 77

    h. divide the total by 7   77 ÷ 7 = 11 with no remainder

    i. no remainder means June 20, 1942, was on a Saturday.

8. Try this with your birth date. Leave the answer in the magic hat. Do you think this magic trick is valuable enough to memorize the three tables?

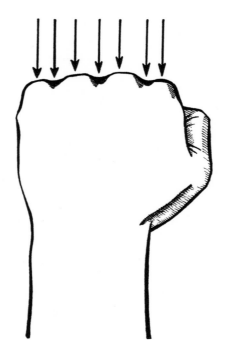

Calendar

Do you have trouble remembering which months in the year have thirty days and which have thirty-one? Many grown-ups have this problem and often must waste time hunting for a calendar.

Here is a super easy way to remember. Make a fist with your left hand and count the months on both your knuckles and the depressions between your knuckles. Call the knuckle of your first finger 'January', the depression between your first and second fingers 'February', your second knuckle 'March' and so on right down the line. You run out of your hand with July so start over again until you reach December.

We all know that counting numbers on our fingers is a very bad habit but there should be nothing wrong with counting months on our knuckles. The interesting thing about this is that all of the months on our knuckles have 31 days while the months that fall between our knuckles have only 30 days. The only exception to this simple system is February, and everyone remembers that February has only 28 days or 29 in leap years.

Super Memory

Here is a 'trick' which will only take about 20 minutes to learn but which will help you to remember things for the rest of your life. It is based on the simple principle that it is harder to forget something than to remember something. If you don't believe that then try to forget your name.

First you must memorize a simple list of 12 words. Here are the words:

1.	*A*pple	7.	*G*host
2.	*B*oy	8.	*H*and
3.	*C*at	9.	*I*gloo
4.	*D*onut	10.	*J*ail
5.	*E*lephant	11.	*K*nife
6.	*F*irecracker	12.	*L*emon

It will just take you a few minutes to learn this list because it is in alphabetical order. This means that 'cat' begins with the letter 'c' and 'c' is the third letter in the alphabet so 'cat' is the third word. The same is true with all of the other words. Should you forget what the 9th word is then just count down the alphabet. The 9th letter is 'i' so nine can't be *h*and or *j*ail but must be *i*gloo.

You must learn these 12 words and their order before you can have a super memory. Have a friend help you practice by giving him a list of the words. First call out the words to him in their proper order, saying the number before each word (one-apple, two-boy, three-cat, etc.). When you can do this pretty fast, then try and call the words backwards (twelve-lemon, eleven-knife, etc.).

Now practice by having your friend call out a number or a word. When he says a number, you tell him the word or when he gives you a word on the list, tell him the number.

Once you have learned these twelve words in their proper order then you will never forget them. Why? Have you forgotten your name yet?

It will now be very easy to remember a list of any twelve words quickly by what is known as 'association'. First, as you repeat each of the words on your list, picture the word in your mind. Don't just say 'apple' as a word but as you say it, picture a big, red, shiny apple in your mind. What is the apple doing? Is it just sitting there?

Now let us imagine that your mother wants you to buy four things at the store. She wants you to buy some hair pins, a bar of soap, a toothbrush and a sponge. Oh, and while you are gone, she wants you to mail a letter. When you were little she probably had to write you a list but now with your super memory you won't need a list. Here is how you make your super memory work:

As she names each thing on her list, you picture it with the objects on your secret list. The sillier and funnier the picture the better.

1 is *apple* and she wants *hairpins* so you picture in your mind a big red apple wearing a silly wig being held in place by giant hairpins.

2 is *boy* and she wants a bar of *soap*. Can you imagine a boy sliding down a giant bar of soap?

3 is *cat* and she needs a *toothbrush*. Picture a grinning cat brushing his teeth.

4 is *donut* and she wants a *sponge*. What can you picture for this?

5 is *elephant* and she wants you to mail a letter. Can you picture a big elephant putting his long trunk into a mailbox and getting it stuck?

This all sounds very silly but can you see how it works? Now you are at the store and you can't remember what your mother wanted. Picture your apple. What is the apple doing? It's wearing a silly wig with giant hairpins. "That's right," you remember, "She wanted hairpins!"

This simple trick can also be helpful in school. Anytime you must remember a list just consult your supermemory. Should you have to learn the parts of a tooth (enamel, dentin, pulp, cementum and gum) just picture an enamel apple, a boy with a 'dent-in' his head, a cat being beaten to a 'pulp', a donut made out of cement, etc.

Math

Instant Math

1. This trick makes you look like an instant calculator but is really quite simple. Give a person several cards with numbers on them and have him think of any number between one and one hundred. He then hands you every card that contains his number. As soon as he gives you the last card you ask him a silly question such as "Do you prefer banana ice cream or strawberry ice cream?"

    No matter what his answer is you then immediately tell him the number he selected.

2. Take seven small sheets of paper or index cards and print the following numbers on them:

A	B	C	D
1 23 45 67 89	2 23 46 67 90	4 23 46 69 92	8 27 46 73 92
3 25 47 69 91	3 26 47 70 91	5 28 47 70 93	9 28 47 74 93
5 27 49 71 93	6 27 50 71 94	6 29 52 71 94	10 29 56 75 94
7 29 51 73 95	7 30 51 74 95	7 30 53 76 95	11 30 57 76 95
9 31 53 75 97	10 31 54 75 98	12 31 54 77 100	12 31 58 77
11 33 55 77 99	11 34 55 78 99	13 36 55 78	13 40 59 78
13 35 57 79	14 35 58 79	14 37 60 79	14 41 60 79
15 37 59 81	15 38 59 82	15 38 61 84	15 42 61 88
17 39 61 83	18 39 62 83	20 39 62 85	24 43 62 89
19 41 63 85	19 42 63 86	21 44 63 86	25 44 63 90
21 43 65 87	22 43 66 87	22 45 68 87	26 45 72 91

E	F	G
16 27 54 81 92	64 75 86 97	32 43 54 97
17 28 55 82 93	65 76 87 98	33 44 55 98
18 29 56 83 94	66 77 88 99	34 45 56 99
19 30 57 84 95	67 78 89 100	35 46 57 100
20 31 58 85	68 79 90	36 47 58
21 48 59 86	69 80 91	37 48 59
22 49 60 87	70 81 92	38 49 60
23 50 61 88	71 82 93	39 50 61
24 51 62 89	72 83 94	40 51 62
25 52 63 90	73 84 95	41 52 63
26 53 80 91	74 85 96	42 53 96

3. These are the seven cards that you hand to your friend. The trick works almost by itself. The silly question that you ask at the end has nothing to do with it. To find the number simply add the numbers in the upper left hand corner of the cards returned. For example if the number were 33 you would be handed cards A and G and you would add 1 and 32.

4. Why does this work? If you can figure it out, write your explanation on a piece of paper and put it in the magic hat.

Good Scouts

One day the Amazing Windley was performing a magic show at a Boy Scout Camp. After the show he was walking along the camp and found seven of the boys fighting. It seems that there were only six tents and each boy wanted a tent of his own. Here is how the magician solved the problem:

He put two boys in the first tent but promised them that it would just be for a few minutes. Then he put the 3rd Boy Scout in tent number 2, the 4th boy in tent number 3, the 5th boy in tent number 4 and the 6th boy in tent number 5. He then returned to the 1st tent and took the 7th boy and placed him in tent number 6. This way each Scout had a tent of his own.

Did the magician really solve the boys problem? Write your explanation on a piece of paper and leave it in the magic hat.

Magic Flower Garden

1. Here is a picture of some boys and girls in a garden. Take a pencil and lightly draw a circle around some of the children.

2. Now take a clean sheet of paper, write your name at the top and use the paper to solve the following magic puzzle.

3. Write down the number of boys you have circled and then multiply this number by 2. Then add 3 to your answer.

4. Now multiply the result by 5.

5. To this add the number of girls that you have circled and multiply the answer by 10.

6. To this add the total number of children that you have circled that are holding flowers.

7. Subtract 150 from your total.

8. Your answer is a three digit number. The first digit is the number of boys you circled above. The middle digit is the number of girls that you circled and the last digit is the number of children you circled that are holding flowers.

9. Can you solve the mystery of why this trick always works? If you can then write your answer on your paper and leave it in the magic hat.

10. Hint: 3 times 5 is 15 and 15 times 10 is 150. This is why you must subtract 150 at the end.

The Missing Domino

Do you know how to play the game of dominos? If you do then you can perform a good trick using a set of dominos.

1. Find a complete set of dominos and spread them out face up on a table.

2. Secretly put one domino in your pocket but make sure that you do not chose a double.

3. Now find two friends and perform this trick with them. Lay out the double six and tell them to build away from it as they would if they were playing a real game. You will go out of the room while they do this and they are to remember the two end numbers when they have used up all the dominos. Then they are to come and get you and you will read their mind and tell them the two numbers.

4. While you are out of the room look at the domino in your pocket. The two numbers on your domino will be the two numbers at the end of their game.

5. You can repeat this trick by slipping your domino back into the set and taking another one. Can you figure out why this trick always works?

The Magic Q

1. Take twelve checkers and lay them on a table in the shape of a 'Q' so that they look like the picture.

2. Have a friend think of a number and tell him that while your back is turned, he is to count that many checkers starting with the end of the tail. Point to checker 'A' to show him where to begin counting. If it is a large number he is to keep counting around the circle until he has reached his number.

3. When he has finished then he is to again count the same number beginning on the checker he last ended but this time is to count backwards (counter clockwise) around the circle.

4. After he has done this you can turn around and point to the exact checker in which he ended his count even though you do not know his number.

5. The secret is easy. No matter what number he thinks of he will always end his count with the checker marked with an 'X' in the picture.

6. Can you figure out why this trick works every time?

Windley Can Read Your Mind

"Hello. I am Windley, the magician, and I am going to try and read your mind. Are you ready?

"Try to follow my directions in your head. If you become confused then you may use a pencil and paper but do not let me see what you write. I shall read your mind and tell you how much money you have in your pocket at this very minute. If you do not know how much money you have then count it before we begin our magic.

"I can see that you do not have very much. We will have to pretend that buttons are money. Count all of the buttons on your clothes and pretend that they are pennies. Add your money and your button pennies together.

"Now take your total and multiply it by two.

"That still isn't very much. Take your answer and add ten cents.

"Good, now you are thinking of a lot of money. Divide the number you are thinking of by two. Then subtract the number that you started with.

"Think of the number of pennies left. I have it! The answer is five!

"Did I fool you with my magic? Like all good magicians, I am not going to tell my secret but if you are a good jr. magician then you will be able to figure it out for yourself."

It's Even Odd

1. Find some checkers and place them on a table. Read all of these instructions and practice this trick first by yourself, then perform it for a friend.

2. Tell your friend that he is to hold some checkers behind his back and that you will turn around and hide your eyes so that you do not see how many he takes. He can take any number that he wants but tell him to remember if he takes an odd or an even number.

3. After he does this, turn around and pick up three checkers and hold them in your hand. Tell your friend that if he took an odd number of checkers the addition of your checkers will make the number even. However if he took an even number then the addition of your checkers will make the total odd.

4. Both of you count your checkers and your friend will see that what you said proves to be correct.

5. Try this trick again but this time you pick up five checkers. Still his odd number when added to yours becomes even or his even number when added to yours becomes odd.

6. Can you figure out how this trick works? Here is another magic trick using the same secret:

7. Tell your friend to hold an odd number of checkers in one hand and an even number in the other hand. Turn your back so that you cannot see how many checkers he picks up.

8. Tell him to multiply the number of checkers in his right hand by two and to multiply the number of checkers in his left hand by three. He is then to add the two totals together and tell you only the sum.

9. Even though you never looked at his hands, as soon as he gives you the total you tell him which hand holds the odd number of checkers and which holds the even.

10. Here is how you know the answer: if his sum is an odd number then the right hand holds the odd number of checkers but if his sum is even then his right hand holds the even number of checkers.

1089

1. Write the number '1089' on a slip of paper and fold it so that no one can read it.

2. Give the slip of paper to a friend and have him put it in his pocket without reading it.

3. Now give him a pencil and paper and tell him to write down any three digit number. It can be any number just so no two digits are alike.

4. Have him reverse the number and subtract the smaller from the larger.

5. Tell him to reverse his answer and add those two numbers together. Ask him to tell you his total and he will say, "1089."

6. Tell him that you predicted his total and let him look at the slip of paper in his pocket.

7. The secret is that the total will always be 1089. Why do you think this is true?

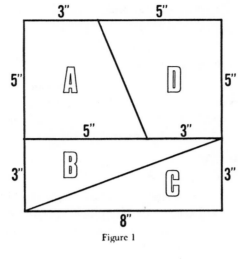

Figure 1

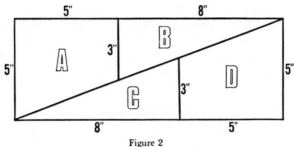

Figure 2

1. We all know that the area of a rectangle is equal to its length times its width. But you know magicians . . . they won't even let the laws of mathematics alone! The Amazing Windley figured out how to make an inch vanish. See if you can discover his secret then you can fool your friends with this magic stunt.

2. Take a piece of cardboard and a ruler and draw a square 8 inches by 8 inches and then cut it out with a pair of scissors. Then, using your ruler to measure, draw lines in the square like those in the picture. Mark the pieces A-B-C-D and cut them out.

3. Reassemble the four pieces back into a square. The total area of the square is 8 times 8 or 64 square inches. Check this yourself with a ruler.

4. Now reassemble the pieces to form a rectangle as shown below in figure 2. The area of this rectangle is 13 times 5—a total of *65* square inches—one more than before!

5. Replace the pieces as in figure 1 and the extra inch vanishes. Where did it come from and where did it go?

6. If you can figure out Windley's secret, explain it on a piece of paper and place it in the magic hat.

Math Whiz

1. You don't have to be a whiz in math to perform this magic but you will sure look like one.

2. With a ruler and a piece of paper make a chart just like the one below, then cut a square from cardboard just large enough to cover four squares.

3. Place the chart on a table and give someone the cardboard. Tell him to cover any group of four squares on the chart. Almost as soon as he does this, you can tell him the *total* of the four numbers that were covered.

4. The total will always be different so you can repeat this trick as often as you like.

5. The secret is easy as the trick works because of the way the numbers are arranged. The magic number for you to remember is 65. When a group is covered, you count *diagonally* two squares from any corner of the cardboard and subtract that number from 65. Your answer will always be the total of the four numbers covered. For example, if the lower right corner is covered (8-25-14-1) you would count diagonally two squares and come to seventeen. 17 from 65 is 48 which is the correct total.

24	11	3	20	7	24	11	3	20	7
5	17	9	21	13	5	17	9	21	13
6	23	15	2	19	6	23	15	2	19
12	4	16	8	25	12	4	16	8	25
18	10	22	14	1	18	10	22	14	1
24	11	3	20	7	24	11	3	20	7
5	17	9	21	13	5	17	9	21	13
6	23	15	2	19	6	23	15	2	19
12	4	16	8	25	12	4	16	8	25
18	10	22	14	1	18	10	22	14	1

6. The last time you present the trick in a different way. Tell your friend to touch any number and you will tell him the total of that number added to the one above and below and the numbers on each side. No matter which one he touches, the total of the five numbers will always be 65.

Perception 5

Little Things

Do you pay attention to little things? One reason that a magician is able to fool people is that most people have never learned to really see with their eyes. They may see big things like a door but they seldom use their eyes to notice what color the door is or what kind of handle it has. Being observant is a very good habit. Do you see with your eyes?

Just for fun, take a pencil and paper and write down the answer to the following questions:

1. Is the name of your school on the front of the building? What color are the letters?

2. What color is the front door to your school?

3. You have seen many pennies and you know that all pennies have a picture of Abraham Lincoln on the front but does he face to the left or to the right?

4. Without looking, what color socks are you wearing today?

Here is a good magic trick with a deck of cards. It works because people do not watch very closely.

1. Take a deck of cards and remove the seven of clubs, the eight of clubs, the seven of spades and the eight of spades.

2. Turn the seven of spades and the eight of clubs over and place them in the center of the deck upside down.

3. Place the other two cards (the seven of clubs and eight of spades) on the table and you are ready to begin the trick.

4. Show your friends the two cards on the table and slowly puch them into the deck, one card near the top and the other card near the bottom, and then place the deck of cards on the table.

5. Tell your friends that you will give the deck a little tap with your finger and cause the two cards to come together. Not only that but you will also cause them to turn over.

6. Tap the deck and have your friend look through the cards. He will set the two face up cards and, because he did not look at the first two cards closely, will think the face up cards are the same ones that he saw you put in the deck.

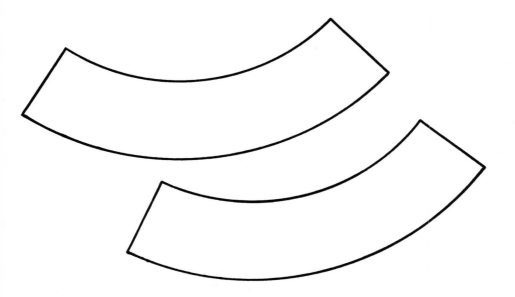

Many magicians can fool your mind but here is a way to fool your eyes. Look at the two bars below and see if you can tell which one is larger. One looks much bigger than the other but if you take a ruler and measure them you will find that they are both the exact same size.

1. For a project take a piece of cardboard and place a sheet of carbon paper over it. Now place this page over the carbon paper and trace over the two bars making an impression on the cardboard.

2. Cut out the two bars from the cardboard and color one red and the other green.

3. Now if you lay the red one on a table and place the green one above it, the red bar appears larger but if you place the green bar below the red then the green bar appears larger.

4. Why do you think this is true?

The Floating Finger

1.   This isn't really much of a serious trick and won't fool anyone but it is silly enough to be a bit of fun.

2.   Hold the tips of your index fingers together at about arm's length and stare beyond them. That is, stare into the distance at the wall across the room and bring your fingers into view without refocusing your eyes. What you will see is a little finger between your two real fingers. If you do not see this at first then bring your hands closer to your eyes until the little finger appears.

3.   Now if you move your fingers apart a little bit it will appear that the middle finger is floating in the air.

4.   This looks even stranger when you try it with your entire hand touching all of your fingers.

5.   Try this with two pencils that are exactly alike. Move the pencils apart and the third pencil appears to float in the air between the other two.

6.   What other objects can you use with this optical experiment?

7.   On a separate sheet of paper, write the definition of the word 'optical' and explain why these magic images appear. Leave your paper in the magic hat.

Free Quarter

1. Give a friend a small sheet of paper and tell him that if he can cut or tear it into four equal pieces within two minutes that you will give him a quarter.

2. Your friend will think this quite easy because all he has to do is carefully fold the paper in half, then in half again and tear the creases. He will always win this simple bet.

3. After he has torn the pieces, compare then and agree that he has done just what you asked him to do.

   "You win," you tell him, "so here is your quarter." With that you hand him one of the four pieces of paper which is now of course a quarter . . . that is a 'quarter' of the piece of paper which is what you were talking about all along.

4. This, of course, can't really be called magic but is just a joke. It shows, however, that sometimes one word can mean different things to different people. In this case you meant you would give your friend a quarter of the paper and he understood you to mean that he would receive twenty-five cents.

5. For a project make a list of things you could say that could have more than one meaning. Leave your list in the magic hat.

Coin through a Ring

We could not speak or make others understand our ideas without words but sometimes these same words can confuse us. Here is a simple trick that sounds impossible but if you read the instructions very, very carefully then you will be able to perform it.

1. You will need a penny, a finger ring, a pencil and a piece of paper. Find these items and place them in front of you and we can begin.

2. Write your name at the top of the paper and then write the name of this trick (Coin through a Ring).

3. Now push the penny through the ring.

4. The secret of how to push the penny through the ring is at the bottom of this page but do not look until you give up. See if you can figure out the secret without looking below.

5. After reading the solution, you will learn that the secret is really quite simple.

6. This, of course, was only a game but do you now see how important words are and that we should be careful how we use them so that others can understand us?

7. On your paper, make up a list of word tricks of your own. Here is another example: Tell a friend that you can stand on one finger. When your friend says that he doesn't believe you because the stunt is too hard, simply bend over and place your finger under your foot. Your friend will laugh because you are doing just what you promised and standing on one finger.

    See if you can make a list of at least ten other word tricks like this and leave your paper in the magic hat.

    The secret is in the way that the stunt is worded. Take the pencil and, placing it through the ring, push the penny along the table. Because the pencil passes through the ring you are *pushing* the coin *through* the ring. Of course it would be impossible to actually make the penny pass through the ring because the ring is too small.

1. This is a good magic trick. Practice it a few times and then try it on your classmates. All you need to perform it is a piece of paper, a pencil and a small empty box.

2. Give a friend the paper and pencil and tell him to think of something very cold such as an ice cube or a cold drink. Turn your back and tell him to write his word at the top of the paper.

3. Next he is to think of something very hot such as fire or the desert and write that in the center of the paper.

4. Finally he is to think again of something very cold and to write that at the bottom of the paper. Keep your back to him so that you cannot see what he writes.

5. When he has finished, tell him to tear the paper into three strips so that he has a word on each strip and to place all three strips in the box.

6. Have him hold the box in the air so that neither you nor he can see inside. Turn around and tell him that you can reach into the box without looking and take out the one piece of paper that has something hot on it. This, you pretend, is because that piece of paper will be warm while the other two pieces will be cold.

7. The real secret is very simple. Because your friend tore the paper, the middle piece with the hot word will have two rough edges while each of the other two strips will have one rough edge and one smooth edge. All you have to do is feel the edges of the paper.

Magic Pennies

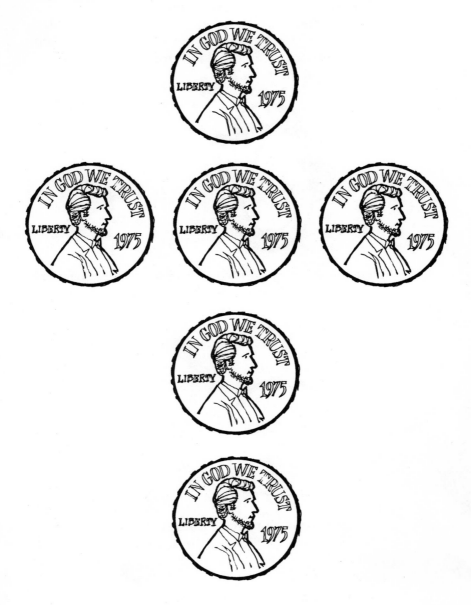

1. Here is a simple puzzle but I bet it will take you a long time to figure out the answer.

2. You need six pennies. Lay them on a table as in the illustration. Now the problem is to rearrange the pennies so that you can count four pennies up and down and four pennies across at the same time. As it is now, you can count four up and down but only three across.

3. If you can figure out the answer, write it on a piece of paper and leave it in the magic hat.

Eye See

1. This poor man has been lost in the desert and hasn't had a drop of water in over a week. You can help him drink the water in the glass by bringing the picture slowly towards your eyes until your nose almost touches the * between the man and the glass. Try it.

2. Here is another magic picture that works the same way. The magician's dove escaped from its cage. Catch the bird and put it back in the cage by slowly touching the * in the picture with your nose.

3. Because our eyes are a few inches apart, they both see the same object from a slightly different angle. This gives us depth perception and is one of the ways in which we can judge how far away an object is from us.

4. Invent your own situation and draw a picture that works like the two above. Sign your picture and leave it in the magic hat.

5. Another interesting trick based on this same principle of perception is to roll up a piece of paper into a tube and look through it with one eye while placing your open hand alongside the tube and looking at your hand with the other eye. It will appear as though you have a hole in the middle of your hand. Try it.

Pin-etration

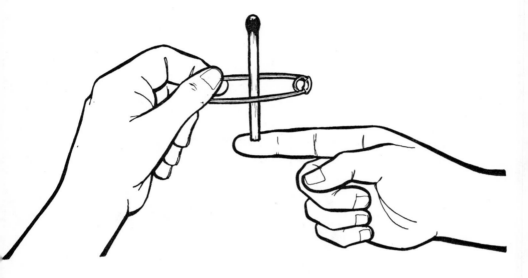

1. Here is an astonishing optical illusion that will probably fool even you the first time you try it. Practice by yourself first and then you will have a neat magic trick to show your friends. You will need a large safety pin and a wooden match provided by your teacher.

2. Push the point of the safety pin carefully through the middle of the match so that the match can revolve freely around the pin. Now close the pin.

3. Hold the safety pin in your left hand like the picture and, with the right finger, turn the match so it is above the pin. With your right finger under the tip of the match lift upward but not hard enough to break the match. Let go of the match by flipping your right finger upward and it will appear as if the other end of the match went right through the safety pin!

4. Of course we know that the match didn't really go through the pin. What actually did happen? Why does it look like the match goes through the pin?

Mental Effect

1. For this mind reading trick you will need a deck of cards.

2. Tell a friend that to find one special card in an entire deck requires a tremendous mental strain on your part so you hope that he won't mind if you relax a bit and try the experiment with just half of the cards. One out of twenty-six is still pretty amazing.

3. Handing your friend half the deck, you tell him to shuffle it and to select any card at random and look at it but not to tell you what it is.

4. After he looks at his card he is to put it into your half of the deck and then shuffle the cards.

5. While he thinks of his card you look through your half of the deck and pull the correct card out and show it to him.

6. The secret of this magic is that you prepared the cards before you performed the trick. In one half of the deck you have all of the clubs and diamonds and in the other half you have all of the hearts and spades. When your friend takes a card from one half and puts it in the other half, it will be easy to find because it will be the only heart or spade in the packet.

7. Arrange your cards for this trick and then try it on a class-mate.

Red and Black

1. This is a good magic trick but must be practiced so that you can perform it well without your audience finding out the secret. You will need two empty match boxes, a red and a black checker and a red and a black crayon or felt tip marker.

2. To perform the magic, you show the items to your friends. You then place the red checker in one of the matchboxes and mark the end of the drawer with the red pen. Now you put the black checker in the other match box and you mark that drawer with the black pen.

3. Place the two boxes on the table and remind your friends of what you did. You placed a red mark on the box with the red checker and a black mark on the box with the black checker. Say some magic words ('rubber baby buggy bumper' are good magic words if you can say them) and slowly open the boxes. Your friends will believe you are a real magician because the red checker is now in the black box and the black checker is in the red box.

4. The secret is pretty easy but it must be performed smoothly to fool people. Before the trick begins, place a red mark on the end of one drawer and a black mark on the other drawer. Open the drawers part way so that the marks are inside the box covers. This way they will not be seen.

5. When performing the trick for your friends, place the red checker in the box with the secret black mark. Place a red mark on the open end and close the box and place it on the table. Do the same with the other checker and the other box.

6. While saying the magic words, pick up both boxes and secretly turn them around in your hand. You can now show the black checker in the box marked red and the red checker in the box marked black.

7. When you open the boxes to show the checkers, leave the boxes open and your friends cannot see the wrong marks.

Skill

Bombs Away!

Some magic is just in knowing the correct way of doing things. Here is a game that you can play by yourself.

1.   Find an old deck of cards and a hat.

2.   Place the hat on the floor and stand next to it.

3.   Hold one of the cards about three feet over the hat and see if you can drop it into the hat. Did it go in or did you miss the hat? Keep trying with the rest of the cards.

4.   There are 52 cards in a deck. How many did you get to fall into the hat?

5.   Take a piece of paper, write your name and the number of cards that went into the hat.

6.   Now pick up the cards and try again but this time hold the cards by the edges so that they fall flat. Write down the number of cards that went into the hat this time.

7.   When held parallel to the floor the cards fall in a straight line but when held perpendicular to the floor they float away. Why is this? Write your answer.

8.   Leave your paper in the magic hat.

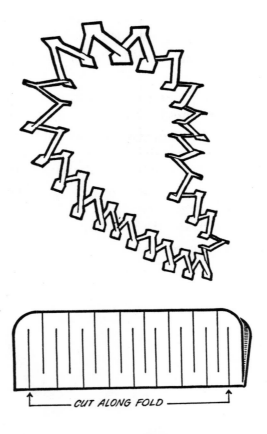

CUT ALONG FOLD

1. Here is an interesting puzzle. Can you cut a hole in a regular playing card so that the hole is big enough for you to step through? The answer is yes. Here's how.

2. Take a playing card from an old deck and bend the card in half lengthwise. Now cut the card as shown in the illustration.

3. After you finish your cuts, open the card and cut along the fold except for the strips on either end. The result is a big chain that stretches large enough for you to step through.

1. Here is a stunt that looks pretty hard but becomes quite easy when you know the secret. You will need a small glass, such as a juice glass. It should be small enough so that you can almost place your fingers completely around it. Also you will need a pair of dice.

2. Hold the glass as shown in the picture. With the middle finger and thumb grasp one of the die (one of a pair of dice is called a die ... the word 'dice' means two) and rest the other die on top of the one that you are holding.

3. Now try to toss the top die in the air by jerking your hand upward and catch it in the glass. This is pretty easy to do.

4. Now for the hard part. Jerk the second die in the air and try to catch it in the glass without the first die falling out.

5. The trick to catching the second die is simply to let go with your fingers and then drop the hand quickly, catching the die as it falls.

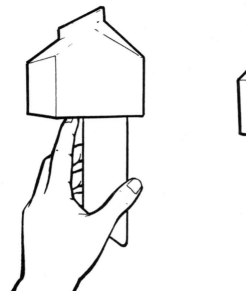 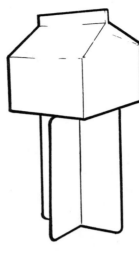

1. Balancing an empty milk carton on a playing card sounds impossible but it is easy if you know the secret. Here are two different ways to perform this balancing trick.

2. The first way is done with an unprepared card. Show your friends a playing card and the empty milk carton and have him try the stunt. No matter how careful your friend is the carton will always fall.

3. Now step back a few feet and try it this way. Hold the card in your left hand by the edges but as you place the carton on top, secretly hold up your index finger so that the carton is sitting on the card *and* your finger. Your friends will not be able to see that your finger is helping because it is hidden by the card. Make sure you are standing back far enough so that no one is to your side or they will see the secret.

4. Another way to perform this balancing act is with a trick card. To make a special card you will need two playing cards and some glue.

5. Fold one of the cards lengthwise and glue half of it to the back of the other card. Wait for the glue to dry. Because you glued only half of the card you now have a card with a secret flap that can open into a tripod.

6. To perform the trick hold the card together so the flap does not show and show both sides of the card. Stand the card on the table by secretly opening the flap in the back and place the milk carton on top. It now looks like you are not only balancing the carton on the card but also making the card balance on the table.

7. Before your friends can get too close and discover the secret to your balancing act, pick up the milk carton with one hand and the card with the other hand, closing the flap as you pick it up.

Color Test

1. You will need five crayons of different colors for this super mind reading stunt. Make sure that they are all about the same size and shape.

2. Give the crayons to a friend and tell him that you are going to try to read his mind. You will turn your back and he is to hand you one crayon and then hide the others behind his back.

3. After he has done this you turn around and face him but still keep your crayon behind your back so that you cannot see it.

4. Tell your friend to concentrate on the color that he gave you. After a few minutes you tell him the correct color.

5. The secret to this magic is really easy but to be effective it requires a bit of acting on your part. All you do is mark your thumb nail with the crayon while you are facing your friend. When you pretend to have trouble reading his mind, point to him saying, "I'm sorry but you are not thinking hard enough."

    As you say this, peek at your thumb nail and you will see the color. Put your hand behind your back again and secretly rub the color off your nail as you tell him which color you are holding.

Spooks Alive!

We all know that there are no such thing as real ghosts but it's fun to pretend. The enjoyment that comes with this mystery is when you explain to your friends that you have a ghost friend that is pretty smart. He can't talk, however, so you have trained him to answer questions in code.

You show your friends a pencil and ask to borrow a finger ring which you place over the pencil. Holding the pencil straight up you explain that Sam (or whatever you wish to name your ghost) will answer questions by lifting the ring to the top of the pencil—once for 'yes' and twice for 'no'.

Your friends then proceed to ask questions and as promised the ring runs up and down the pencil giving the correct answers.

1. First you will need a long wooden pencil, a needle and a piece of thin black thread. You should also have a ring available in case your friends do not have one of their own.

2. Thread the needle and then push it through the eraser of the pencil. Now remove the needle and tie the thread so that it stays in place. The other end of the thread, which should only be about 18 inches long, is either tied to the middle button on your shirt or to your belt buckle. Now the pencil can be placed in your shirt pocket and you are ready to begin.

3. As you explain about the ghost to your friends, take the pencil from your pocket and hold it in front of you by the point.

4. Borrow a ring and drop it over the pencil. Of course it also goes over the secret thread. If the light isn't too bright and if you are wearing rather dark clothes, the thread will be invisible. It also helps to hide the thread if your friends stand back a few feet. Explain to them that if they get too close then the ghost will become frightened and may run away.

5. The ring will rise when you slowly move the pencil away from your body because of the tightening of the thread. Bring the pencil close to you and the ring will fall again.

6. This would be a good way to practice your school work. Give your friends a spelling word and have them spell it. The 'ghost' can tell them if they spelled it correctly or not. Of course, since you are controlling the ring you will have to know how to spell the words yourself also.

Jumping Rubber Band

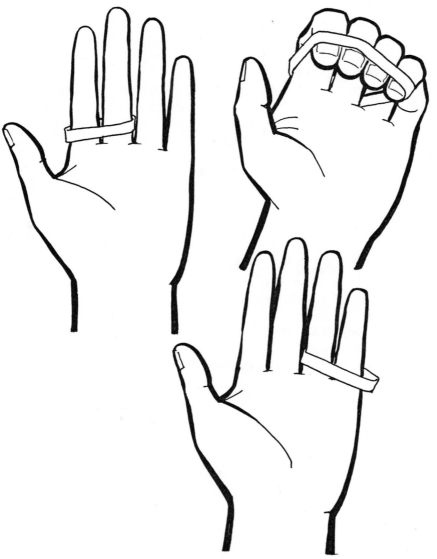

1. All you need to perform this magic is a rubber band and your right hand. The audience will see you place the rubber band around the first two fingers of your hand but at your command it will jump to the other two fingers.

2. To perform the magic you actually place the band around the base of your first two fingers and show your friends.

3. Now while holding the back of your hand towards your friends, make a fist with your hand.

4. As you make a fist, place the inside part of the band around the tips of all four fingers. Because the back of your hand is towards your friends they do not see you do this.

5. Now all you have to do is open your hand and the rubber band will jump to the other two fingers.

Producing a Rabbit

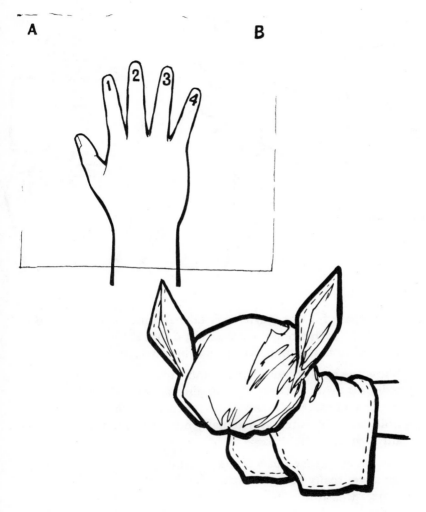

People are always asking magicians to produce a rabbit, but no magician wants to secretly carry a live rabbit around with him all day. The Amazing Windley solves the problem by producing a rabbit puppet made from a pocket handkerchief. Here is his secret.

1. First place the handkerchief over your right hand as in the picture. Bring corner 'A' under your hand and slip it between your third and little finger.

2. Next take corner 'B' and slip it between the thumb and first finger. Pull both corners up tightly and they become the rabbit's ears.

3. Now make a fist with your right hand and the handkerchief will look just like a rabbit face. Have the rabbit peek over your left arm and you can do a little show.

4. If you wiggle your fingers it will look like the rabbit is wiggling his nose. You can make him look happy or sad or even shy.

Coin through a Card

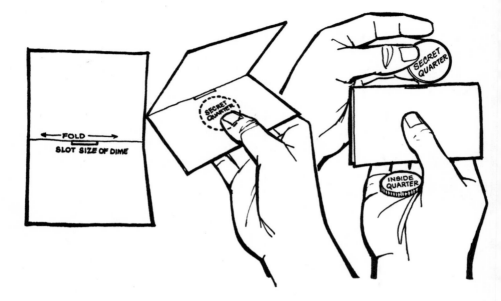

1. To prepare for this magic trick take an index card and fold it in half, then along the crease cut a thin slit just wide enough so that a dime will easily slip through it.

2. Show the card to your friends and show them how a dime will pass through the hole. Explain that with the help of magic you can also make a quarter fit through the same hole. As they watch you actually push a real quarter through the little slot.

3. The secret is easy but will take a bit of practice. The quarter never really goes through the hole but you can make it appear that it does by secretly using two quarters.

4. When you begin the trick, have a second quarter hidden under the card. It is held in place by the middle finger of the right hand as you hold the card. With the left hand show the first quarter and place it on top of the card and fold the card over it. When the card is closed, press your thumb on the card over the quarter so that it will not slide.

5. Now tilt the card so that the slit is down and with the bottom fingers slide the secret coin along the bottom of the card until it sticks out where the slot is located.

6. Grab the quarter with the left hand and pretend to pull it through the hole. Then raise your right hand so that the slot points upward, relax the pressure on the inside quarter and it will secretly slide into your right hand where no one will see it.

7. You can now pass the quarter and card to your friends but of course they can't do it because they do not know the secret.

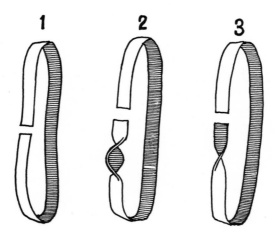

Here is a mystery that is used on stage by many professional magicians. What you will do is show your friends a large loop of paper. The paper is about an inch or two wide and about three or four feet long. With a pair of scissors you cut the paper lengthwise, going all the way around the loop. When you finish you end up with two loops. Not much magic since you simply cut the big loop in half.

Now the magic comes. You take another loop and again cut around it but this time instead of two separate loops, the two loops are somehow linked together!

"Quite easy," you tell your friends. "Here is another loop and the scissors. You try it." Now your friends take the loop and cut the same way but when they finish they don't end up with two loops linked OR unlinked but have one giant loop!!!

1. The secret is in the way you prepare the loops of paper before the experiment. Take a five or six foot length of adding machine paper and paste the ends together to make a circle. When you cut this you will end up with two separate loops.

2. Take another piece of adding machine paper and make a loop but this time give the ends a complete twist before pasting them together. When this loop is cut the rings will be linked together.

3. Now take another piece of paper but before pasting only give the ends half a twist. This paper will end up being one large circle.

4. Try this by yourself, then make up another set and fool your friends. Remember not to tell your friends the secret or you will spoil the magic.

Creativity 7

Your Nose Knows

Here is a super magic stunt that you can perform for several of your friends.

1. Give someone ten checkers and have them place the checkers in a straight line on a table.

2. Tell the person to point to any one of the checkers while you are out of the room and that when you return you will be able to tell which one he selected.

3. Leave the room (or if that is too much trouble just turn your back so that you can't see) until the checker has been chosen.

4. Explain that you have a magic nose and that you can sniff the checker that was chosen. To make the magic more fun you can even make up a funny story as to why you have this special talent. Perhaps you learned the secret from a cocker spaniel?

5. Bend over and sniff a few of the checkers then point to the one that was selected. Your friends will be amazed and will wonder how you knew.

6. You can try the experiment many times and each time you will be able to tell which checker was selected when you weren't looking.

7. The secret is really easy and has nothing at all to do with your nose. Before performing this magic, all you have to do is arrange with a friend to secretly signal you when you sniff the checker that was selected.

8. You and your friend must decide the best signal and then keep that signal a secret. He could signal you by shouting "That's it!" but everyone would hear him and then would know how the trick was done. He could signal you by winking his eye but that too would be risky as someone may notice him. Suppose he just smiled slightly or wet his lips with his tongue? See what kind of secret signal you and your friend can come up with that no one will discover.

Solar Energy

1. You will need a piece of paper, a pair of scissors, a piece of string and a lamp with a strong bulb such as 100 or 150 watts for this experiment.

2. Draw a spiral on the paper and then cut it out.

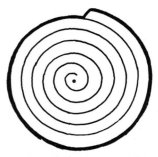

3. Tie the center of your spiral to the string and hold it over the light and it will spin around. Which direction does it spin?

4. Explain on a piece of paper why the paper spins and place it in the magic hat.

5. Try this with different colors of paper. You will notice that some colors spin faster than other colors. Why is this?

6. It is also fun to play with shapes. What happens when the following shapes are cut from paper and held over the light?

7. See if you can design a super fast spiral. Put your name on your fastest spiral and leave it in the magic hat. On a special day perhaps your instructor can line up several lamps and have a race.

One Line Pictures

1. Here are some simple drawings:

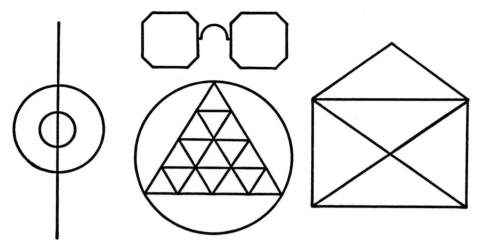

2. Take a piece of paper and copy each drawing.

3. Now draw the pictures again but this time draw each picture without lifting your pencil from the paper, crossing a line or retracing a line.

4. Could you do them all? Just for fun see if you can design a picture that can be made with only one line. Sign your paper and leave it in the magic hat.

Using Magic

Magic secrets can often be used for practical purposes in everyday life. Once Windley, the magician, was on a camping trip with some scouts and showed them how to make a burner for their camp stove using just three table knives. With the help of a simple principle of *structural engineering*, the three knives were used to support each other's weight. Here is how he did it:

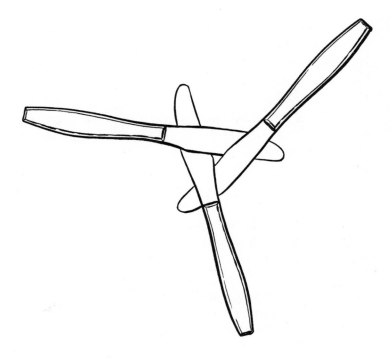

Take three dull table knives and rest them on each other. Knives placed like this can support the weight of a glass of water or, in the case of the camping trip, a small pot for cooking.

Windley was quite surprised when later he found the boys playing baseball. The lot was muddy but one of the boys had used Windley's principle with three bats to make himself a seat.

What practical uses can you come up with using this simple principle of structural engineering? Leave your suggestion in the magic hat.

The Sex Detector

Here is an experiment that could almost be called real magic! I say 'almost' because every mystery has an explanation or reason for happening even if human beings have not yet fully uncovered the answer.

1. For this experiment you will need a weight such as a metal fishing sinker tied to a piece of string. The string should be about seven or eight inches long.

2. Hold the string in front of you so that the weight hangs perfectly still without moving. This works best if you are standing and it is important that your arm is completely free—that is, you shouldn't have your arm resting on a table.

3. Hold the weight several inches over a girl's hand or over her head if she is sitting down and you will notice that the weight slowly begins to swing in a circle going around and around. It will be hard to notice at first but soon the circle will become wider and wider and the weight will swing faster and faster.

4. Now hold the weight over a boy's hand and this time the weight will again move but rather than travel in a circle it will swing back and forth in a straight line.

5. Why does the weight always swing in a circle when held over a girl and in a straight line when over a boy? The only scientific explanation is that the person holding the string knows how it should move and without realizing it makes it go in the correct direction.

6. To carry the experiment further—and this is the really interesting part—the person holding the weight can be blindfolded and it will still work. Try this by blindfolding yourself and having a member of your group hold their hand under the weight. Even though you do not know whose hand it is, the weight will still swing correctly. Could this be ESP or real mind reading? No one as yet really knows the answer.

The Magic Word

1. Read all the directions before trying this magic on one of your classmates.

2. Give your friend a book and have him choose a page by telling you a number. Then have him choose a word by giving you another number. For example if he says 24 and 9 then tell him to take the book and look up the 9th word on the 24th page. He is to do this while you are out of the room.

3. After he has done this you come back into the room and tell him the word.

4. The secret to this magic is easy. You need two copies of the same book. Keep one book in your hand and hide the other book somewhere outside of the room.

5. After your friend chooses two numbers—one for the page and the other for the word—go out of the room while he looks up the word on that page.

6. While you are out of the room secretly look up the word yourself in the book that you have hidden. When you return, you can pretend to read your friends mind and tell him the correct word.

7. You can repeat the trick with another word on another page but remember not to let anyone know your secret.

Holidays 8

FIVE PROJECTS:

1. Halloween
2. Thanksgiving
3. Christmas
4. April Fools' Day
5. Washington's Birthday

Halloween

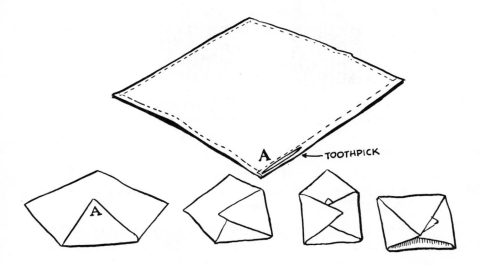

Halloween is a special day of monsters and goofy ghosts. Here is a super magic way of creating a ghost of your very own.

1. All you will need for this magic is a pocket handkerchief and a toothpick.

2. Carefully push the toothpick into the hem of the handkerchief near the corner. This will make the corner stiff but the toothpick will not be seen. This is your secret 'ghost'.

3. To perform this magic for your friends, show the handkerchief to your audience and lay it on a table with the toothpick corner closest to you. Now fold corner 'A' (with the toothpick) over so that the corner is in the center of the handkerchief. Repeat this with the other three corners.

4. Show your hand to be empty and then reach into the handkerchief above the toothpick but under the other three corners.

5. As you say some magic words, stand the toothpick straight up and down then carefully remove your hand. There will now appear to be a large lump in the handkerchief.

6. To prove that the 'ghost' is really there, take a solid object such as a book or a ruler and tap the handkerchief. If you are careful to hit the toothpick squarely on the top it will make a 'thump' and really look like there is a big solid object in the handkerchief.

7. You can make the ghost go away by grabbing the top corner and flipping the handkerchief in the air!

Thanksgiving

Thanksgiving began in this country with a big feast that the Indians and Pilgrims celebrated together in honor of the harvest. Although today we go to the store to buy our turkeys for Thanksgiving dinner, the Pilgrims had to hunt for theirs. Here is how you can prove to your friends that you would have been a super turkey hunter.

1. Take a piece of green construction paper and cut out five circles of the same size. An easy way to do this would be to find a big jar lid and draw around it. With crayons, color the discs to look like trees.

2. Now take a piece of yellow paper and cut one circle that is a little bit smaller than the green ones. On this yellow disc draw a picture of a turkey.

3. Now for the secret. Pull just one hair from your head. You will need a hair that is about one inch long. Glue one end of the hair to the edge of the turkey (yellow) disc and you are ready to perform the magic.

4. Show the turkey and trees to your friends. Have them hide the turkey under one of the trees while your back is turned. When you turn around to look, you can tell which tree hides the turkey by secretly looking for the hair which will be too long for the green disc to cover. The hair is so thin that it won't be noticed by your audience.

Christmas

Here is a magic Christmas card that you can make. In addition to sending holiday greetings to your friends and family, you can provide them with a neat puzzle.

1. Using heavy construction paper, trace the following three figures and then cut them out.

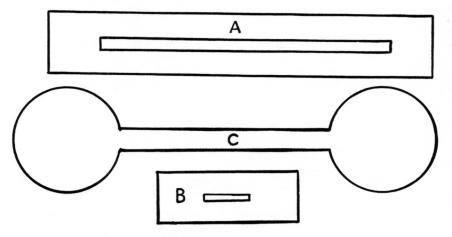

2. Now bend the wreath in half, decorate the pieces with crayons and assemble as follows: Bend piece 'A' in half but do not crease. Slide piece 'B' over the bottom of piece 'A' and then place the wreath around piece 'B' as in the picture.

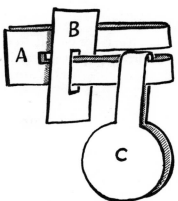

3. Now carefully slide piece 'B' on to the top of the wreath and open piece 'A'. This is what you should have:

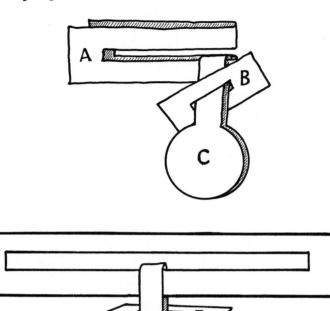

4. The problem, of course, is for people to figure out how in the world you put the three pieces together. Few people will be able to figure out how to take the three pieces apart again.

April Fools' Day

April Fools' Day is a fun day on which we play jokes on our friends, but we always want to be very careful that we do not play jokes that may hurt anyone. A good test would be to ask ourselves if the victim of our April Fool prank will laugh with us when the joke is finally discovered.

Here are some silly April Fool jokes that are both harmless and fun:

1. Show your friend a pencil and tell him that it is a new kind of pencil that will write any color. When he says that he doesn't believe you, simply write the words 'red', 'blue', 'green', 'yellow', etc. Then smile and say "April Fool!"

2. To make a glass of warm water look like a glass of ice water, crumble a small piece of transparent plastic such as the kind candy is wrapped in and place it in the glass. The plastic in the water looks just like crushed ice.

3. On the back of this page is a picture of the most horrible monster you will ever see. Don't look at it if you don't like to be frightened.

4. What April Fool joke can you think up to play on your friends?

April

Fool!

Washington's Birthday

George Washington is remembered as the father of our country. In addition to being our first president, he was also a great general during the American Revolution. Here is an interesting experiment that you can try with the picture of Washington below:

1. Stare at the picture below and slowly count to fifty. You must stare with both eyes directly at his nose in the center of the picture.

2. Now immediately look at a black spot on a lightly colored wall and after about ten seconds a large picture of Washington will magically appear on the wall. The longer you look at one spot on the wall, the clearer the picture will become.

3. When the picture begins to fade, blink your eyes rapidly and it will return.

4. The secret to this magic picture is what is known as 'eye retention.' When you stare at something dark for a long time (such as the black in the picture) it takes a few minutes for the image to fade away.

Appendix

THE FOLLOWING SHOULD BE HELPFUL to teachers in selecting projects for specific students. This list should also be consulted for a summary of materials needed for each project.

SECTION 1 *—SEVEN PROJECTS—Fun*

Houdini, Jr.—p. 19   materials—string

This can be used several ways. The entire class could be paired off with a contest or game to see which couple solves the problem first or with just two students at the Magic Center challenged to figure out one of Houdini's secrets. The solution is not on the project sheet but is as follows:

For clarity let us say that a boy and girl are tied together. The boy takes the center of *his* string and pushes it up and through one of the loops that is around the girl's wrist, then brings it down over her hand.

Strong Man—p. 20   materials—paper napkins or paper towels and a glass of water

A simple stunt for one student to learn alone, then perform for others.

The Magic Rolling Crayon—p. 21 materials—several round crayons

Project for one student to learn alone, then perform for others.

Four Aces—p. 22
A simple card trick for one student to learn alone, then perform for others.

materials—a deck of cards

Defying Gravity—p. 23
Project for one student to learn alone, then perform for others.

materials—dull, metal table knife, paper cup, small magnet

The Magic Balloon—p. 24
Project for one student to learn alone, then perform for others.

materials—several round balloons (number 7 or 9 balloons work best), several straight pins, roll of cellophane tape

The Genie in the Bottle—p. 25
Complex stunt for one student to learn and prepare alone, then perform for others.

materials—soft drink bottle either pre-painted inside or supplied with paint for student to accomplish depending upon age and skill of student. Also one foot of rope (window cord sash available by the foot at hardware stores), small cork or ball about ½" dia. (available in yard goods or fishing dept. of dime store) and several paper drinking straws

SECTION 2—*TWELVE PROJECTS—Science*

The Floating Needle—p. 29
For one student alone.

materials—bowl of water, package of sewing needles

Poof!—p. 30
For one student to do alone. The secret that the student is seeking is static electricity.

materials—drinking glass (a thin glass goblet works best), paper matches (without striking surface), nickel, pocket comb (hard rubber comb better than plastic)

Falling for Science—p. 31
For one student to do alone. The student is presented with a problem but no solution. The solution is to place the paper disc on top of the coin and, holding the coin flat, to drop both together. The coin then reduces the air resistance for the paper.

materials—half dollar, paper, scissors

How to Make a Rainbow—p. 32
   Project for one student to do alone.

materials—2 sheets of clear glass such as the glass from picture frames, a glass of water, a candle in holder and means to light candle

Spilling the Beans—p. 33
   For one student alone.

materials—empty soda bottle, dried beans (from grocery store) and one large, wide, flat bangle bracelet (from dime store)

Salt and Pepper—p. 34
   For one student to try alone.

materials—salt and pepper in shakers, glass of water, comb

Looping and Ice Cube—p. 35
   For one student alone. Solution is for student to lower the string so that it rests on the ice, then sprinkle common table salt on the cube. Wait until the salt makes the ice melt and then refreezes around the string before lifting the cube out of the water.

materials—glass of water, string, ice cube, salt

The Magic Match—p. 36
   For one student alone, then to perform for others.

materials—several large wooden kitchen matches (be sure to burn match heads for safety), 2 pair pliers, 2 small scraps of cloth

The Sword and the Stone—p. 37
   For one student to perform alone, then for others. The reason this project works is that by sealing the far end of the straw, no air can escape when the other end is driven into the potato. The air becomes compressed and keeps the straw rigid.

materials—several raw potatos, several plastic drinking straws

The Dancing Egg—p. 39
   For one student alone.

materials—rubber band, glazed or glossy paper (page from quality magazine will work), a large glass or jar, (several raw eggs, bowl, straight pin)

Rolling up a Hill—p. 40
For one student alone.

materials—2 large books, spool of thread, 2 like funnels, glue, cardboard, scissors

The Mysterious Button—p. 42
For one student alone, then to perform for others.

materials—glass of soda water, small shirt button

SECTION 3—*FOUR PROJECTS—Memory*

Colors—p. 45
For one student to learn alone, then perform.

materials—paper, scissors, red, white, blue, yellow, green, and black crayons

Remember That Day—p. 46
Teaches bright students how to calculate exact day of the week that any date falls upon. For one student alone.

materials—none

Calendar—p. 48
For one student alone.

materials—none

Super Memory—p. 49
For one student alone, then with helper. Teaches student easy system for remembering lists.

materials—none

SECTION 4—*TEN PROJECTS—Math*

Instant Math—p. 53
One student alone, then for audience.

materials—index cards, pen

Good Scouts—p. 54
For one student alone.

materials—none

Magic Flower Garden—p. 55
For one student alone.

materials—none

The Missing Domino—p. 56
For one student alone, then to perform with 2 classmates.

materials—set of dominos

Appendix

The Magic Q—p. 57
For one student alone, then for audience.

materials—checkers

Windley Can Read Your Mind—p. 58
One student alone.

materials—none

It's Even Odd—p. 59
First alone, then for group.

materials—checkers

1089—p. 60
First alone, then for audience.

materials—none

The Vanishing Inch—p. 61
For one student alone.
NOTE: By definition, the corners of a rectangle must be right angles. Look at fig. 2 on the project sheet and you will see that corners A & D are right angles but the other 2 corners although appearing to be right angles cannot be so proven and are therefore *not* right angles so you really haven't got a rectangle at all. Thus the mysterious *square* inch doesn't exist.

materials—cardboard, carbon paper, scissors, pen, ruler

Math Whiz—p. 62
Alone, then for audience.

materials—paper, pen, ruler, scissors

SECTION 5—*ELEVEN PROJECTS—Perception*

Little Things—p. 65
First alone, then for audience.

materials—deck of cards

Optical Illusion—p. 66
For one student alone.

materials—cardboard or construction paper, carbon paper, scissors

The Floating Finger—p. 67
For one student alone.

materials—none

Free Quarter—p. 68
For one student alone, then for one friend.

materials—piece of paper

Coin through a Ring—p. 69
For one student alone.

materials—coin, finger ring, pen

Hot and Cold—p. 70
For one student alone, then for one friend.

materials—paper, pen

Magic Pennies—p. 71
For one student alone. The solution is to pick up coin 'A' and place on top of coin 'B'.

materials—6 pennies

Eye See—p. 72
For one student alone.

materials—none

Pin-etration—p. 74
For one student alone.

materials—large safety pin, wooden match (be sure to burn match head for safety) or use safety matches

Mental Effect—p. 75
For one student with one helper.

materials—deck of cards

Red and Black—p. 76
For one student alone, then for audience.

materials—2 empty match boxes, red and black checker, red and black crayon

SECTION 6—TEN PROJECTS—Skill

Bombs Away—p. 79
For one student alone.

materials—deck of cards and a hat or small box

Walking through a Playing Card—p. 80
For one student alone.

materials—several playing cards, scissors

Galloping Dice—p. 81
For one student alone.

materials—pair of dice, small juice glass or paper cup

Balancing Fun—p. 82
For one student alone, then for audience.

materials—empty school milk carton, old playing cards, glue

Color Test—p. 84
For one student to learn alone, then try before audience.

materials—new box of crayons

Spooks Alive!—p. 85
For one student alone, then to perform for audience.

materials—finger ring, wooden pencil, black thread, needle

Jumping Rubber Band—p. 86
For one student alone.

materials—several rubber bands

Producing a Rabbit—p. 87
For one student alone.

materials—pocket handkerchief

Coin through Card—p. 88
For one student to perform for audience.

materials—index card, 2 coins, scissors

To the Loop—p. 89
For one student to learn alone, then perform for audience.

materials—adding machine paper, glue, scissors

SECTION 7—SIX PROJECTS—*Creativity*

Your Nose Knows—p. 93
For *2* students to learn, then perform for audience.

materials—checkers

Solar Energy—p. 94
One student alone or this would make a good class project after your lecture on solar energy.

materials—paper, scissors, strong lamp

One Line Pictures—p. 96
One student alone.

materials—none

Using Magic—p. 97
For one student alone.

materials—none

The Sex Detector—p. 98
For several students.

materials—string, fishing weight, blindfold

The Magic Word—p. 99
For one student alone, then with a friend.

materials—2 copies of the same book

SECTION 8—*FIVE PROJECTS—Holidays*

Halloween—p. 103
For one student alone, then for audience.

materials—pocket handkerchief and toothpick

Thanksgiving—p. 104
For one student alone, then with a friend.

materials—green and yellow construction paper, crayons, glue, short human hair

Christmas—p. 105
For one student alone.

materials—construction paper, scissors

April Fools' Day—p. 107
One student alone.

materials—none

Washington's Birthday—p. 109
One student alone.

materials—none

NOTE: The above materials list assumes that paper and pen are always available at the Magic Learning Center.

The Magic Hat

AN IMPORTANT PART OF THE Magic Learning Center is the magic hat explained elsewhere in this book as it is the 'hat' that will contain the results of a student's efforts and/or conclusions with a project.

In order to save you time, below is a list of the projects that use the magic hat.

SECTION 1—*Fun*
    The Magic Rolling Crayon

SECTION 2—*Science*
    The Floating Needle
    Poof!
    Falling for Science
    Salt and Pepper
    The Sword and the Stone
    Rolling up a Hill

SECTION 3—*Memory*

SECTION 4—*Math*
    Good Scouts
    The Vanishing Inch

SECTION 5—*Perception*
    The Floating Finger
    Free Quarter
    Coin through a Ring
    Magic Pennies
    Eye See

SECTION 6—*Skill*
    Bombs Away

SECTION 7—*Creativity*
    Solar Energy
    One Line Pictures
    Using Magic

SECTION 8—*Holidays*

Index

Acknowledgements

For this book, I would like to offer my sincere thanks to:

Max, my third grade afternoon school bus driver. It was on Thursday, 31 October 1950, that Max cut a length of clothesline in two pieces and then completely restored it. I remember nothing else of my third year in school.

Earl H. Edwards, a magician in Norfolk, Virginia, who taught me the secret of that rope trick along with the workings of thousands of other mysteries.

Every school child in Virginia, Maryland, Washington, D.C., New York, Pennsylvania, Florida, and North Carolina who has attended my performances of "Wonderland of Magic" from 1959 until the present time when it was presented in their school auditorium.

Ralph Voight,* who witnessed his students' reactions to my show and discovered its value as a learning center.

*(Author of *Invitation to Learning, Vol. I: The Learning Center Handbook* and *Vol. II: Center Teaching with Instructional Depth,* Acropolis Books Ltd., $4.95 each, quality paperback.)